DONT LOOK BACK—the most searching and intimate portrait
of Bob Dylan that has appeared in any medium.

"FANTASTIC . . . There is an intense aura about Dylan, an
electric, almost anarchistic excitement generated by him and
about him. Perhaps more than any other modern young
artist, Dylan is the spokesman for the new society. . . . Here
we are given Dylan's world, an existentialist riddle world of
philosophy, blues, hard rock, and poetry. 'I'm just a guitar
player,' he said, but he is really a classic troubador, the town
crier for the young world, announcing that the times have
changed."

—Gene Youngblood, *LOS ANGELES HERALD-EXAMINER*

BOB DYLAN

DONT LOOK BACK

D. A. PENNEBAKER

To Sylvia and Sara

Designed by Carol Inouye

This is not the script from which DONT LOOK BACK was made. The film was made without a script. This is simply a transcript of what happened and what was said. It is as accurate as the fallible human ear can make it. It is no substitute for the reality of the film. Since that sense (of reality) is missing (it explains itself on film), it is necessary to tell something of the conditions under which the film was made.

A sort of complicated game. Neither side quite knows the rules. The cameraman (myself) can only film what happens. There are no retakes. I never attempted to direct or control the action. People said whatever they wanted and did whatever. The choice of action lay always with the person being filmed. Naturally, I edited the material as I believed it should appear, but with the absolute conviction that any attempt to distort events or remarks would somehow reveal itself and subject the whole to suspicion. The order of the film is almost entirely chronological and nothing was staged or arranged for the purposes of the film. It is not my intention to extol or denounce or even explain Dylan, or any of the characters herein. This is only a kind of record of what happened.

D. A. Pennebaker,
New York, 1968

This book, as well as the film it represents, happened many years ago, nearly forty, which is a long time for a book, film, or particularly a person to remain pivotal to the public eye. But, surprisingly, through all these years Dylan has continually beguiled our imaginations. His story seems timeless.

D. A. Pennebaker,
New York, 2006

DONT LOOK BACK had its first performance at the Presidio Theater in San Francisco on May 17, 1967. On September 6 of that year it opened in New York City at the 34th Street East Theater.

ITINERARY
for
Dylan's Concert Tour of England, 1965

Sheffield . . . . April 30
Liverpool . . . . May 1
Leicester . . . . May 2
Birmingham . . . . May 5
Newcastle . . . . May 6
Manchester . . . . May 7
Royal Albert Hall, London . . . . May 9 & 10

Contents

PART 1

PART 2

Homesick Blues

Dylan stands in an alley. He holds large lettered cards. He throws these down as the song "Subterranean Homesick Blues" is played.

Johnny's in the basement
Mixing up the medicine
I'm on the pavement
Thinking 'bout the government
The man in the trench coat
Badge out, laid off
Says he's got a bad cough
Wants to get paid off
Look out kid, it's somethin' you did
God knows when
But you're doin' it again
You better duck down the alleyway
Lookin' for a new friend
The man in the coonskin cap by the pig pen
Wants eleven dollar bills
You only got ten.

Maggie comes fleet foot
Face full of black soot
Talkin' at the heat put
Plants in the bed but
The phone's tapped any way
Maggie says that many say
They must bust in early May
Orders from the D.A.
Look out kid
Don't matter what you did
Walk on your tip toes
Don't try "No Doz"
Better stay away from those
That carry around a fire hose
Keep a clean nose
Watch the plain clothes
You don't need a weather man
To know which way the wind blows.

Get sick, get well
Hang around a ink well
Ring bell, hard to tell
If anything is goin' to sell
Try hard, get barred
Get back, write braille
Get jailed, jump bail
Join the army, if you fail

Look out kid, you're gonna get hit
But users, cheaters
Six time losers
Hang around the theatres
Girl by the whirlpool
Lookin' for a new fool
Don't follow leaders
Watch the parkin' meters.

Ah, get born, keep warm
Short pants, romance, learn to dance
Get dressed, get blessed
Try to be a success
Please her, please him, buy gifts
Don't steal, don't lift
Twenty years of schoolin'
And they put you on the day shift
Look out kid they keep it all hid
Better jump down a manhole
Light yourself a candle, don't wear sandals
Try to avoid the scandals
Don't wanna be a bum
You better chew gum
The pump don't work
'Cause the vandals took the handles.

PART 1

You Start Out Standing . . .

DYLAN   *sings in dressing room.*
     You will start out standing . . .
Strums guitar.

DYLAN   Did you see my cane?

PENNEBAKER   Yeah, it was right here.

DYLAN   It's gone. You didn't see it, did you?

NEUWIRTH   What?

DYLAN   My cane.

NEUWIRTH   Shit.

DYLAN   It's gone . . . It's not there . . . I left it right there.

GROSSMAN   When? Today?

DYLAN   Uh huh.
Wanders into other room.
     It's in back of this door.

GROSSMAN   He's got it.

DYLAN   It's in back of this door, here. Will you remember?
Goes on stage and door closes behind him.

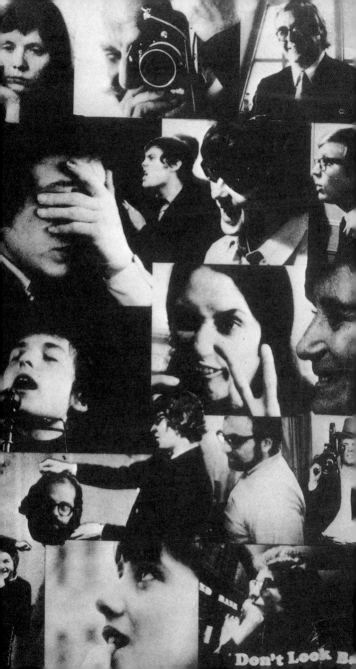

Don't Look B

THE CAST

DYLAN *sings.*
>   I ain't lookin' to compete with you,
>   Beat or cheat or mistreat you,
>   Simplify you, classify you,
>   Deny, defy, or crucify you,
>   All I really want to do
>   Is baby be friends with you.
> As he sings the following names appear.

BOB DYLAN	ALAN PRICE
ALBERT GROSSMAN	TITO BURNS
BOB NEUWIRTH	DONOVAN
JOAN BAEZ	DERROLL ADAMS

LONDON, 1965

*Dylan accompanied by his manager, Albert Grossman,
and his road manager, Bob Neuwirth, arrives at London
Airport. As they walk up the ramp towards the waiting room
Dylan and Neuwirth sing:*

> London Bridge is falling down
> Falling down
> Falling down
> London Bridge is falling down
> My fair Liza . . .

YOUNG MAN
AT GATE   You came here two years ago.

DYLAN   Uh, yes I did.

YOUNG MAN   What's the reason for the change this time?
Why are you so big this time? What do you think?

DYLAN   I've absolutely no idea. I don't even know about
it if it is. I figure just do the same thing I did before.
*Enormous crowd, held back by police, greets him as he
enters airport.*

THE PRESS CONFERENCE

In waiting room at London Airport.

DYLAN   Well, what's happening here? What are we going to do?

REPORTER   How long is it since you were last in London?

DYLAN   About a year.

REPORTER   What's the lightbulb for?
Dylan holds up an enormous industrial lightbulb.

DYLAN   What's the lightbulb for? I thought you would ask me that. No, I usually carry a lightbulb. Somebody gave it to me, you know.

REPORTER   Sorry, I didn't quite catch the answer.

DYLAN   Someone gave it to me . . . a very affectionate friend.

REPORTER   Oh, I see.

2ND REPORTER   *to Bob Neuwirth.*
   Are you folk?

NEUWIRTH   Who, am I folk? No, not me. I'm not folk.

3RD REPORTER   *to Dylan.*
   What is your real message?

DYLAN   My real message? Keep a good head and always carry a lightbulb.

REPORTER   Have you tried it?

DYLAN   Well, I plugged it into my socket and the house exploded.

In room at Savoy Hotel.

GIRL REPORTER   Do you think that a lot of the young
    people who buy your records understand a single
    word of what you're singing?

DYLAN   Sure.

GIRL REPORTER   You reckon they do?

DYLAN   Sure.

REPORTER   Why do you say they do?

GIRL REPORTER   How can you be so sure?   They're quite
    complicated songs, aren't they?

DYLAN   Yeah, but they understand them.

GIRL REPORTER   How do you know they understand them?
    Have they told you that they do?

DYLAN   They told me. Haven't you ever heard that song
    "She Said So . . ."

GIRL REPORTER   *laughing.*
    You've got it wrong.

REPORTER IN
BACKGROUND   Do you think that they understand you
    because they don't want to see you?
Dylan ignores this question.

GIRL REPORTER   Would you say that you cared about people particularly?

DYLAN   Well, yeah, but you know . . . I mean, we all have our own definitions of all those words . . . care and people.

GIRL REPORTER   Well, but surely we know what people are.

DYLAN   Do we?

REPORTER WITH
MICROPHONE   You sound angry in your songs. I mean, are you protesting against certain things you're angry about?

DYLAN   I'm not angry. I'm a delightful sort of person.
Girl reporter smiles.

REPORTER WITH
MICROPHONE   I see, thank you very much.

DYLAN   Okay.

GIRL REPORTER   *leans over and whispers to Dylan.*
Do you ever read the Bible?

DYLAN   What about the Bible?

GIRL REPORTER   Do you ever read the Bible?

DYLAN   Um . . . no.

GIRL REPORTER   Have you read it?

DYLAN   Have I ever? I've glanced through it . . .

GIRL REPORTER   Because you see, a lot of the things you say . . .

DYLAN   I've glanced through it. I haven't read it.

PHOTOGRAPHER *to Joan Baez.*
Hold your hands up to your face.

JOAN BAEZ *in false accent.*
Like that? Well, as I was saying to him, I says . . .
Laughs, says in her normal voice
I can't pose.

PHOTOGRAPHER No, but you don't have to pose, but just do it.

BAEZ I can't do it.
Makes faces.

PHOTOGRAPHER *laughing.*
We publish these things, you know. They'll shake you, you know. Your name, please.

BAEZ Joan Baez.

PHOTOGRAPHER Joan? . . .

BAEZ *spelling out last name.*
B . . A . . E . . ZED.

PHOTOGRAPHER Oh, 'ods truth.
Laughs nervously.
I didn't recognize you, I'm sorry.

BAEZ Good.
Everyone laughs.

26

PHOTOGRAPHER It's nice to see you. I've been looking for you all day.

General laughter.

DYLAN *to reporter.*
This is the part where I don't write. You know, anything that happens I'll just remember, you know. When I'm living my own thing, doing what I do, this is never around me. I mean, I accept everything. I accept this, you know, I'll accept...

REPORTER Why?

DYLAN Well, because it's here, cause it's real, cause it exists just as much as the busses outside exist. I mean, I can't turn myself off to it because if I try to fight it you know, I'm just going to end up going insane faster than I eventually will go insane... if I do go insane... when and if the time comes for me to... go... in... sane.

Photographer snaps picture.

27

Who's This Donovan?

DYLAN *reading newspaper story about himself.*
Puffing heavily on his cigarette, he smokes eighty
a day. God, I'm glad I'm not me.

BAEZ *sings to Sally Grossman, who stands in doorway,*
holding a rose.
Sally go 'round the roses
Sally don't tell your secret,
Sally don't tell your secret.
Roses they can't hurt you
Roses they can't hurt you.

BAEZ You know that song, Sally?

SALLY GROSSMAN Yeah, I like that.

DYLAN   *still reading newspaper.*
Donovan. Who's this Donovan? Let's put him right out on the sidewalk.

NEUWIRTH   Let's take a look at him.

ALAN PRICE   He's a good guy.

DYLAN   I'd like to meet him.

PRICE   He's a young Scottish bloke. That's how I was going to say that but neither of you would understand. Bloke.

DYLAN   Bloke.
Experiments with the word.   Blooke ya blooke.

PRICE   He's a singer. A bit of folk music, and he's been around and he plays a very good guitar. He's a very good guitar player. He's better than you.

DYLAN   Right away I hate him.
Grins.

PRICE   He's all right. I like him anyway. He's not a fake.

DYLAN   Yeah.

PRICE   He's all right.

DYLAN   Well, I got him up on the wall, you know, anybody on my wall . . .
Gestures to picture of Donovan that has been put up on mirror.

PRICE   Where? Where?

DYLAN   He's right there.

PRICE   "Is Donovan deserting his fans?" He's only been around for three months.

DYLAN   Well, that's what I call a loser.
Baez laughs loudly.

Later.

Dylan record on phonograph.

> *I ain't gonna work for Maggie's brother no more*
> *No, I ain't gonna work for Maggie's brother no more*
> *Well he hands you a nickel*
> *He hands you a dime*
> *He asks with a grin*
> *If you're having a good time*
> *Then he fines you every time you slam the door*
> *I ain't gonna. . . .*

Baez and Price sit in the middle of room as Dylan and Neuwirth continue to tear out pictures from magazines and put them on the wall.

BAEZ   In the South, forget it, you know.

PRICE   In London, forget it.

BAEZ   How can you say that. They've done so much.

PRICE   Oh, yeah. In a short time, that's America. We're talking about England.

BAEZ   No, not in a short time. It's taken twenty-six years.

PRICE   When did Abraham say, "Well, we're equals" and all that, you know? When was the Declaration?

BAEZ   That was 200 years ago.

Price gulps first from gin bottle, then from bottle of orange mixer.

Entering CBS press party.

PRICE   Where we going? To CBS, huh?

Points to doorman.

> He's not with us.

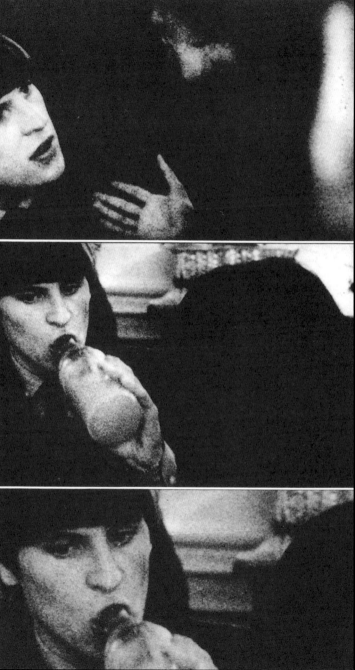

DYLAN He's not with us. We're all thin, he's fat.
Inside.

COLUMBIA RECORDS
OFFICIAL I've got an award for him for the most
    promising artist of the year, and the best selling folk
    record, "Free Wheeling."

DYLAN No, man, I just don't want it.

GROSSMAN Should we have it mailed to you?

DYLAN I don't even want to see 'em.

GROSSMAN OK, all right.

DYLAN Tell them to give it to Donovan.
*Party in full swing. Dylan and Neuwirth sit in back of room,
snapping their fingers to the music, in an exaggerated
imitation of a nightclub singer. Dylan opens paper and
sees picture of Donovan.*

DYLAN Donovan, Donovan, our next target. He's our
    target for tomorrow.

How Did It All Begin

Dylan reading in hotel room.

BBC REPORTER   This is for the African service of the BBC, Mr. Dylan, West African listeners, and it's going out this evening, and the questions are four in number for your approval before we ask them. The first one's a very general, journalistic one. Just how did it all begin for you? What started you off, what triggered it off? Just how do you see the art of the folk song in contemporary society? Has it a very real social impact? Something that will certainly interest our listeners in Africa, Bob, is your deeply humanitarian attitude to a number of public matters. For instance, you're quoted as saying, "People talk about Negroes as if they were objects." Now, does this sort of compassion on your part present any problems for you in America?

DYLAN   Okay.

BBC REPORTER   Oh, by the way, you took part in a play in Britain some time ago written by a school friend of mine, Evan Jones.

DYLAN   Oh, yeah?

BBC REPORTER   Ev and I went to school in Jamaica together. "The Castle Street," wasn't it?

DYLAN   "The Mad House on Castle Street."

BBC REPORTER   Going ahead in, about say, five seconds from now with this interview with Mr. Bob Dylan for the African Service of BBC. Pete Meyers and Colin Weild producing in approximately five seconds.

Pause.

ow did it all begin for you, Bob. What actually started you off?

Times They Are

DYLAN   *sings to a group of Negroes and civil rights*
     workers in Greenwood, Mississippi.
DYLAN   *sings.*
     From the poverty shacks he looked from
     The cracks to the tracks
     And the hoofbeats pound in his brain
     And he's taught how to walk in a pack
     Shoot in the back,
          With his fist in a clinch
          To hang and to lynch
          With his head 'neath a hood
          To kill with no pain
          Like a dog on a chain,

A-Changing

He ain't got no name
But it ain't him to blame,
He's only a pawn in their game.

The day Medgar Evers was buried from
The bullet he caught
They lowered him down as a king
But when the shadowy sun sets on the one
That fired the gun,
You'll see by his grave
On the stone that remains
Carved next to his name
His epitaph plain
He's only a pawn in their game.

Applause: turns into opening night audience at Sheffield Hall Concert.

DYLAN *sings.*

> Come gather round people wherever you roam
> And admit that the waters around you have grown
> And accept it that soon
> You'll be drenched to the bone.
> If your time to you is worth saving
> Then you'd better start swimming
> Or you'll sink like a stone
> For the times they are a-changing.

Dylan tunes guitar in dead silence of hall.

DYLAN *sings.*

> Ramona, come closer
> Shut softly your watery eyes
> The pangs of your sadness will pass
> As your senses will rise . . .

Manchester Guardian reporter in phone booth.

MANCHESTER GUADIAN REPORTER   Sentence. He is not so much singing as sermonizing, colon, his tragedy perhaps is that the audience is preoccupied with song, paragraph, so the bearded boys and the lank haired girls, all eyeshadow and undertaker makeup—applaud the song and miss, perhaps, the sermon. They are there, colon, they are with it. Sentence. But how remote they really are from sit-ins and strikes and scabs and life. Paragraph. "The times they are a-changing" sings Dylan. They are when a poet and not a pop singer fills a hall.

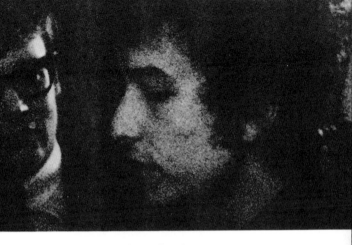

Young men talk to Dylan in hotel room:

QUESTIONS   Are you aware of the fact that tonight at the
City Hall here you had a greater audience than has
been seen there for many years? And more
appreciation than has been heard there. The applause
was fantastic. I never heard so much applause there,
and I've been coming here for quite a while.

DYLAN   That makes me feel good. You know. . . .
Pauses and turns away.

That makes me feel good.

QUESTIONS   Are you religious?

DYLAN   Uh, well, I don't know. What does that mean?
Religious. Does it mean you bow down to an idol or go
to church every Sunday, or that kind of stuff?

QUESTIONS   Do you believe in . . .

DYLAN   I don't believe in anything. No, why should I
believe in anything? I don't see anything to believe in.

QUESTIONS   Are you cynical?

DYLAN   No, I'm not cynical. I just don't—you know. I can't
see anything anybody's offered me to believe—that
I'm going to believe, put all my trust and faith in, and
everything. Nothing is sacred, man.

43

Hotel manager enters, accosts Grossman.

HOTEL MANAGER   Who's in charge?

GROSSMAN   In charge of what?

HOTEL MANAGER   Who is in charge of this room?

GROSSMAN   What do you mean "Who's in charge of this room?" It's rented to Bob Dylan. What do you mean, who's in charge of it?

Dylan appears in doorway.

HOTEL MANAGER   Are you Bob Dylan's manager?

Neuwirth moves in front of Dylan protectively.

GROSSMAN   Yes, I'm Bob Dylan's manager, but I'm not in charge of his room.

HOTEL MANAGER   No, you're in charge of Bob Dylan?

GROSSMAN   No, I'm not in charge of Bob Dylan.

HOTEL MANAGER   We have had complaints about the noise—above, below.

GROSSMAN   Oh, that's unfortunate. We'll try to hold it down.

HOTEL MANAGER   And if it isn't organized in five minutes, I will ask you to leave.

GROSSMAN   Why don't you get a constable—would you please?

HOTEL MANAGER   I will.

GROSSMAN   Please do that. There's been no noise in this room, and you're one of the dumbest assholes and the most stupid persons I've ever spoken to in my life. If we were someplace else I'd punch you in your goddam nose—you stupid nut. Would you . . . we've rented this room and I'm asking you to leave this room. We have valuables in here and I don't want you in here.

Dylan smiles at camera.
> Would you get out of this room?

To Assistant Manager
> You get out of this room also. Don't worry about your
> fop manager.

In car, traveling to Liverpool.
Fred, the tour manager, unfolds paper.

FRED, TOUR MANAGER   As soon as we get clear of the
town we'll be. . . there's one in there . . . shall I read
it now?
Reads from newspaper.

"American folksinger, Bob Dylan, sat scowling in a
hotel armchair last night. In his hands was an iris.
Bob, who arrived 90 minutes before his British tour was
to open at Sheffield City Hall, said he wanted to rest.
Asked to pose quickly for a relaxing picture, he seized
a flower from a vase in the room and said 'This is how
I like to relax. I've been through all this in the States.'
The harsh-rasping, haranguing voice of self-styled
guitar strumming poet Dylan started off his show with
'*The Times They Are A-Changing.*' They certainly are.
This, swears my seventeen-year-old son, is what the
kids who used to scream at the Beatles now go for.
And, if Dylan is a trend, not just a cult, parents need
not be quite so condescending. His tour opening at the
2700-seat hall was a sellout, but without one single
scream and with every . . . rapt attention to every
word. It was very impressive. Alone . . . Dylan, alone
with his guitar and mouth organ for an hour and a
half, earned himself more than 2000 pounds and a
footstamping ovation." That's all.

47

*Carol and two friends wait outside Dylan's hotel in
Liverpool. Carol puts fingers in mouth and whistles loudly.*

FIRST FRIEND   You be staying here tonight at the hotel.

2ND FRIEND   Where?

1ST FRIEND   Near that little theatre.

2ND FRIEND   By the hotel? We both are.

1ST FRIEND   Is that him?

CAROL   No.

1ST FRIEND   Oh, hell.

CAROL   Isn't he handsome? Isn't he lovely?
       Pinch me, pinch me.

1ST FRIEND   Come down.

CAROL   Oh, me dream's come true . . . oh. . . .
Backstage at theatre.

CAROL   Are you going to sing "Times They Are
       A-Changing?"

DYLAN   You want me to sing that, huh? You really like
       that song?

CAROL   Yeah, it's fantastic.

DYLAN   What do you like about it?

CAROL   I don't like "Subterranean Homesick Blues."

DYLAN   Oh, you're that kind. I understand right now.

CAROL   It's not you, it doesn't sound like you at all. It sounds as if . . .

DYLAN   But my friends, my friends, were playing with me on that, though. You know, I have to give some work to my friends, you know. I mean, you don't mind that, right?

CAROL   No.

DYLAN   Huh? You don't mind them playing with me if they play the guitar and drums and all that kind of stuff, right?

CAROL   But it just doesn't sound like you at all, it sounds as if you're having a good old laugh.

DYLAN   Well, don't you like me to have a good old laugh once in a while? Isn't that all right with you?

CAROL   If you're not taken seriously and commercialized.

DYLAN   I don't care. You know different, tho, right? As long as you know, you don't have to worry about anybody else. All the people take care of themselves.

CAROL   Do you have any brothers or sisters?

DYLAN   Huh?

CAROL   Do you have any brothers and sisters?

DYLAN   God, I don't even know that.
Girls giggle.
I have lots of brothers and sisters . . . lots.

FRIEND   I've got a little sister, she's my only one.

DYLAN   Is this called Merseyside?

CAROL   Yeah.

DYLAN   *walks on stage and begins to sing.*
  Come gather round people wherever you roam
  And admit that the waters around you have grown
  And accept it that soon you'll be drenched to
  The bone. . . .

VOICE   *backstage whispers*
  What the hell's wrong with the mike? You can't hear
  him.

FRED   What the hell's happened?

STAGE HAND   No sound here at all.

STAGE HAND   Okay.

STAGE HAND   Well, nobody's pulled anything out except
  that one.

STAGE HAND   Oh, for crying out loud. Come on. Is he
  down there?

FRED   Is he down there? . . . Is he down there?

Sound system suddenly comes on, audience applauds,
Dylan continues to sing.

    . . . The battle outside raging
    Will soon shake your windows
    And rattle your walls
    For the times they are a-changing.

Dylan, Grossman and Sally Grossman drive to concert at
Leicester. Dylan, in front seat, appears asleep.

DYLAN ON RADIO   *sings.*
    For the times they are a-changing.

RADIO ANNOUNCER   Bob Dylan in the number sixteen
    slot with his own composition entitled "Times They Are
    A-Changing."

DYLAN   What number was the other one?

GROSSMAN   What?

DYLAN   What number was the other one?

GROSSMAN   Thirty-one on the "FAB" chart.

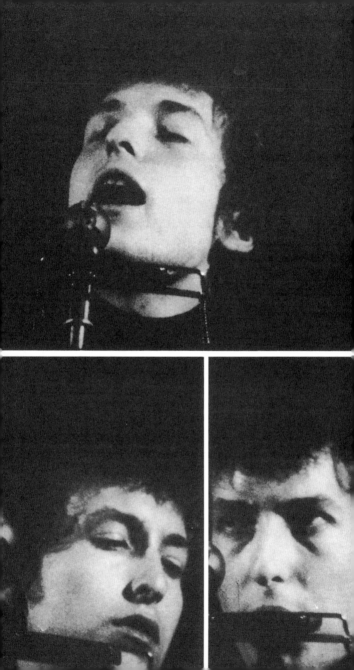

I Just Go There and Sing 'Em

Hall at Leicester. What at first appears to be a hall jammed with people turns out to be only the rear of the stage. The hall itself is even more crowded.

DYLAN *adjusts guitar, tries it a few times, and starts to sing.*

> William Zanzinger killed poor Hattie Carroll
> With a cane that he twirled 'round his
> Diamond-ringed finger
> At a Baltimore hotel society gathering
> And the cops were called in
> And his weapon took from him
> As they rode him in custody down to the station
> And booked William Zanzinger for first degree murder.

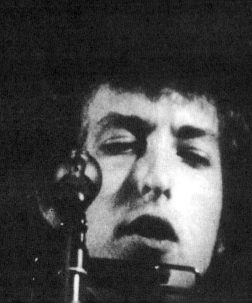

And you who philosophize disgrace
And criticize all fears
Take the rag away from your face
Now ain't the time for your tears.

William Zanzinger, who had just 24 years
Owns a tobacco farm of six hundred acres
With rich wealthy parents
Who provide and protect him
In high office relations in the politics of Maryland
Reacted to his deed with a shrug of the shoulders
And swear words and sneering
And his tongue it was snarling
And in a matter of minutes on bail was out walking
And you who philosophize disgrace
And criticize all fears
Take the rag away from your face
Now ain't the time for your tears.

Hattie Carroll was a maid of the kitchen
She was fifty-one years old
And gave birth to ten children
Who cleaned up the table and hauled out the garbage
And never sat once at the head of the table
And didn't even speak to the people at the table
Who just cleaned up all the food from the table
And emptied the ashtrays on a whole other level
Got killed by a blow, lay slain by a cane
That sailed through the air
And came through the room
Doomed and determined to destroy all the gentle
And she never done nothing to William Zanzinger.
And you who philosophize disgrace
And criticize all fears
Take the rag away from your face
Now ain't the time for your tears.

After the concert a young rock 'n' roll band talks to Dylan
in his dressing room.

1ST MUSICIAN   We do about twenty, thirty of your
    numbers.

DYLAN   Oh, really?

1ST MUSICIAN   We give them all a big band sound, you
    know.

2ND MUSICIAN   You probably wouldn't like it. You'd
    think we ruin them all. We're doing it because we're
    doing it because we're such great . . . such . . . idols
    of you.

DYLAN   Thank you. Are you playing around anywhere?

2ND MUSICIAN   Yeah. When we play anywhere we try
    and tell them it's the words they ought to listen to and
    not the . . .

DYLAN   You play rhythm guitar and electric guitar?

2ND MUSICIAN   Yeah, we play electric guitar.

1ST MUSICIAN   We find it very difficult to get people to
    listen to words tho. What they want to do is just
    listen to . . .

DYLAN   It's beyond me, you know. I just go out there and
        sing 'em, you know. If the people thought I was
        equipped to play . . . I just go out there and sing 'em.
        I'm not going to try to get anybody to listen.
Leaving hall. Crowd is held back by policemen.

NEUWIRTH   Hey, hey, hey.

POLICEMAN   Step out of me way.

CROWD   Bless his heart.

DYLAN   Goodbye, goodbye. I'll see you now. See you
        later.
Crowd bangs on car.

PENNEBAKER   Watch out, watch out, hey, this chick. . . .

SALLY   Hey, this chick is on the back of the car.

DYLAN   There's a guy on our car. Will you get him off?

SALLY   Get that . . . take off . . . take off. . . .

DYLAN   Stop, Bobby. Hey, Bobby tell the guy to stop.

SALLY Hey, she's gonna get hurt.

NEUWIRTH It's a chick. . . .

GROSSMAN It's a. . . .

SALLY It's a girl. . . .

DYLAN Will you take that girl off our car, please? Will
     you please take her off the car? Hey, we gotta get her
     off. Hey, will you get that girl off our car? Oh, she's
     off, she's off. Hey, okay, how you doing? We'll see
     you later, bye.

Turn, Turn, Turn

Drive through rain back to London. Baez starts to sing.

> Bad news, bad news came to where I sleep,
> Turn, turn, turn again. . . .

In hotel room,

> . . . Saying "One of your friends is in the trouble
> deep," turn, turn to the rain and the wind.

*Grossman reads letter, Dylan types, Mary Ann
Faithful listens in chair.*

> "Tell me the trouble, tell me once to my ears,"
> Turn, turn, turn again,
> "It's Joliet Prison for ninety-nine years"
> Turn, turn to the rain and the wind.

Dylan types determinedly.

> "Tell me once how this came to be,"
> Turn, turn, turn again,
> "It was manslaughter in the highest degree"
> Turn, turn to the rain and the wind.

> Sat down and wrote the best words I could write,
> Turn, turn, turn again,
> Asked the judge to see me on Wednesday night
> Turn, turn to the rain and the wind.

Dylan stops writing—listens to Baez sing.

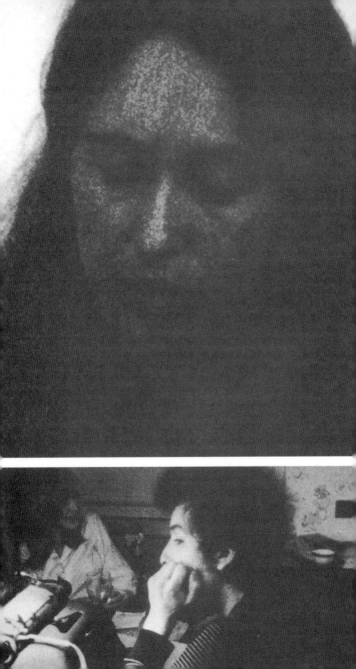

Without a reply I left by the moon
Turn, turn, turn again,
I was in the judge's chambers by the next afternoon
Turn, turn to the rain and the wind.

"Tell me now" I asked without fear
Turn, turn, turn again,
"How one of my friends could get ninety-nine years"
Turn, turn to the rain and the wind.

"A crash on the highway threw a car into a field"
Turn, turn, turn again,
"Four people killed with him at the wheel"
Turn, turn to the rain and the wind.

Baez changes to a new song.

DYLAN   You still remember that goddamned song. . . .

BAEZ   *sings.*
    That love is just a four-letter word.

DYLAN   I never finished that song, did I, huh?

BAEZ *sings.*

    Outside a rattling storefront window
    Cats meowed to the break of day
    Me I kept my mouth shut too
    I had no words to say.

Dylan, Grossman, Mary Ann listen . . .

BAEZ *sings.*

    My experience was limited and underfed
    And you were talking while I hid
    To the one who was the father of your kid.
    You probably didn't think I did, but I heard
    You say that love is just a four-letter word.

    I went on my way unnoticed
    When pulled into my own games
    In and out of lifetimes unmentionable by name
    Searching for my double, looking for
    Complete evaporation to the core
    Though I tried and failed in finding any door
    I probably thought there's nothing more absurd
    Than that love is just a four-letter word.

BAEZ   Do you remember any more, Bobby?

DYLAN   No, I never finished it.

BAEZ   Oh God, you finished it about eight different ways.

DYLAN   Yeah . . . yeah, that's a good song.

BAEZ   Oh, it's beautiful. If you finish it I'll sing it, on a record . . . or something . . .

DYLAN   Yah, well I'll finish it. Have you heard "She Died For Love At Three A.M." Huh? Bill Anderson wrote it.

NEUWIRTH   Hey, you know what's a great song? You remember that song "In The Shadows Of The Warm Red Wine"?

BAEZ   *singing in background.*
   As long as I remember
   She'll remain the rose of my heart. [1]

DYLAN   "Long, Black Veil." Sing "Long Black Veil."

[1] FAMILY REUNION, by Hank Williams, © MCMLVIII by Acuff-Rose Publications Inc. Used by permission of the Publisher. All rights reserved.

NEUWIRTH *laughs.*
>   Hey, don't sing it . . .

BAEZ *continues singing.*
>   *Mom took sick along in December,*
>   *February brought us broken hearts.*

DYLAN Sing "Long Black Veil." She walks these hills in a
long black veil.

DYLAN *Baez harmonizing with him.*
>   *I was just a lad nearly twenty-two,*
>   *Neither good nor bad, just a kid like you.*
>   *Then I got lost, too late to pray . . .*
>   *I started going down that lost highway.*
>
>   *Now, boys, don't start to ramble 'round.*
>   *On this road of sin are you sorrow-bound.*
>   *And you'll get lost till you curse the day*
>   *You started going down that lost highway.* [2]

NEUWIRTH Oh, no, no, no, it's another verse—"I'm a
rolling stone."

DYLAN

Baez still harmonizing.

> I'm a rolling stone, I'm alone and lost.
> For a life of sin I've paid the cost.
> Take my advice, you'll . . .

loses words . . .

> You'll curse the day
> You started going down that lost highway.

DYLAN   Oh, what about . . .

sings.

> Hear that lonesome whippoorwill
> Sounds too good to cry . . .
> That midnight train just rolled away,
> I'm so lonesome I could cry. [3]

NEUWIRTH   Welcome home. It's the first time that this room hasn't been full of a bunch of insane lunatics, man, that I can remember.

BAEZ   Bobby, it was almost so nice, you don't know.

NEUWIRTH   Yeah, it's the first time it's been cool around here.

BAEZ   Oh, God, I'm sleepy, I mean, I'm fagging out.

NEUWIRTH   Let me tell you sister, you fagged out a long time ago—Sheherazade.

Baez puts veil over face.

> You fagged out before you even thought you were faggin' out. Oh, my God, there she is, Fang. Fang, you have one of those see-through blouses. Hey, she has one of those see-through blouses that you don't even wanna. *(laughter)* That's Fang Baez. You wouldn't hurt his guitar, would you?

BAEZ Oh, pardon me.

NEUWIRTH I didn't mean to hurt your turtle.

BAEZ God.
Leaves, closing door behind her.
Neuwirth plays guitar, Dylan types. It is 2:30 in the morning.

BIRMINGHAM

Dylan, John Mayall and Baez drive to Birmingham. Dylan
reads newspaper headlined, "Dylan Digs Donovan."

BAEZ *sings.*
>   You must leave now, take what you need
>   You think will last.

Dylan puts down newspaper and starts to write words to song for Baez.

DYLAN Do you have some more paper where I can write out these things here?

MAYALL I'm afraid you'll have to make the most of that.

DYLAN Really? You don't have any more? Oh, God.

BAEZ *sings, while eating banana.*
>   Yonder stands your orphan with his gun.

Dylan continues to write.

BAEZ *sings.*
>   Crying like a banana in the sun.

Dylan looks up, Baez continues eating banana.
Birmingham. Sign at Birmingham Hall announces "Come and hear the challenge of Bible students."

In dressing room.

BAEZ   sings.
    Here it comes, here
    comes the night.
In outrageous falsetto voice . . .
    Ooooohhh

NEUWIRTH   I wish I could
    sing like that.
Laughter and muffled joking.
    Neuwirth rolls on floor
    laughing.

DYLAN   *puts his hand over his*
    ears and groans.
    No . . . No . . .

NEUWIRTH   Long live
    Queen Lucy.
In high falsetto voice. Then,
    in heavy midwest accent.
    Mighty pleased to be here,
    crown my daughter queen
    of this here azalea festival.
In his normal voice.
    Did you see that, man,
    the cat got on the platform,
    reached into his pocket,
    pulled out a speech
    and said,
in accent
    "So happy to be here."
Everyone laughs.
Fred enters and silently calls
    Dylan for concert.

NEUWIRTH   Want to do it now?
    Oh, yeah, concert. I knew
    we were here for some
    reason. I knew it wasn't
    a hotel.
Laughter. Do good.

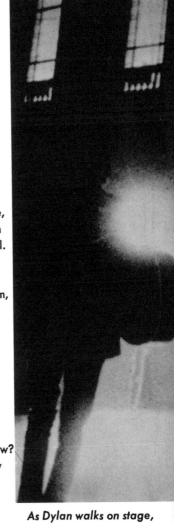

As Dylan walks on stage,
door closes after him.

71

Denmark Street

London home of agents and music publishers. Grossman sits in office of Tito Burns, British Producer.

GROSSMAN   Now, what kind of money do you think?
   How far do you think we can push them?

TITO BURNS   I tell you. As far as Granada goes, uh,
   they were talking 12-13 hundred pounds but there's
   15 hundred there, I know.

GROSSMAN   You don't think we can do better?

TITO BURNS   Possibly, yeah. But I know that like he's
   talking to us 13. . . .

GROSSMAN   Why don't we ask for 2,000?

TITO BURNS   *laughs.*
   Well, I had that figure in mind, strangely enough.

GROSSMAN   *doesn't laugh.*
   Get it settled.

BURNS   Great.

GROSSMAN   Why don't we, why don't we hear now
   and get an answer from them . . . 'cause you know
   why, don't you? Just tell them that I have to present it
   to Bob before we can give them the final answer,
   but we'll give it to them by tomorrow.

BURNS   Fine . . . I'll get Johnny Hamp, Granada in there.
   The other one was rediffusion, but they're the same.
To secretary.
   Uh, Johnny Hamp, please. Urgently, wherever he is.
   Track him down, dear.
To Grossman.
   The top one so far really is Granada, but I haven't
   spoken to him.
Phone rings.

SECRETARY   *on intercom.* Umm, Johnny Hamp is in the
   studio, his secretary's there. If she could have some
   idea of what it's about she might be able to
   get him to come to the phone.

BURNS   Just say Bob Dylan. He'll be there in a shot.
To Hamp. Two grand, Johnny. Yeah, on an exclusive.
        And it would be very much exclusive. He's not
        going to do anything else. Yeah . . . yeah . . .
        yeah . . . yeah . . . you want to leave that with you,
        John? Hello?

CHRIS   *On phone at other end.* Hello.

BURNS   Yes.

CHRIS   Ah, this is Chris, Stewart's P.A. speaking. He's
        not there. He's not, he's not, you know, available at
        the moment. He's a bit tied up in the theatre.
        Can I help?

BURNS   Well, I think he might untie himself. Would you
        tell him this is the call he was expecting
        regarding Bob Dylan?

CHRIS   Bob Dylan?

BURNS   Yes.

CHRIS   OK, well you know, when I say he's tied up
        I really mean it. You know, I'm not kidding.

BURNS   I know he is . . . with rope, right?

CHRIS   No, look, we've got a show on in the theatre here,
        you know?

BURNS   Don't get upset, don't get upset—I'm only
        kidding ya.

CHRIS   OK, well I'll try and get him.

BURNS   Well, you tell him, Chris, that I have Mr. Grossman
        with me. Uh, Bob's manager, Albert Grossman's
        with me now.

CHRIS   OK.

BURNS   OK? Bye . . . how 'bout that? Thinks I'm
    tryin' to put him on.
To Stewart on phone. Stewart? Ummmm . . . yeah . . .
    yeah . . . uh huh, oh dear. That for the two?
    Hmmm might go to 15. I see. Uh, fine. Well, I'll
    tell you what I'll do. Yeah, not bad for me, I'll take
    it for a week's work. I don't mind. Uh, Stewart,
    look, shall I just check this out with Albert now and
    sit down there and . . . to save you from hanging
    on? And then give you a call back? God bless you.
To Grossman.
    1250. You could probably get him to stretch it to
    fifteen hundred. So, I figure this, you know, BBC, ah . . .

GROSSMAN   One show, but not for two.

BURNS   No. I had a feeling that Granada would
    come up with the money because they have done in
    the past. Remember what he offered Peter, Paul &
    Mary for two shows BBC. For two that seems
    to be their, their top.

GROSSMAN   If you get him back, why don't you leave
    me take a crack at him on the phone.

BURNS   Pleasure.

GROSSMAN   'Cause he called me in the states, you know.

BURNS   Who . . . Stewart or Johnny?

GROSSMAN   Stewart.

75

BURNS   Stewart? . . . Listen Stewart, I've got
         Mr. Grossman for you. Will you hold on a second?

GROSSMAN   I spoke to you in New York, didn't I?
         Uh, remember. Yeah. And uh, at that time I indicated,
         uh, the kind of money we were looking for . . .
         for Bob and I assumed that when Tito told me you
         were interested that we were somewhere in that
         vicinity and that I was personally, you know,
         kind of you know, surprised, you know, at, you know,
         the nature of the offer. In other words, as much
         as we'd like to do the show for BBC I think we can't
         even consider it at that money 'cause it doesn't
         come anywhere near the other offers that we have.
         OK, well the minimum that I would consider would,
         uh, be the fee that you mentioned for each
         half hour. No, no, no—I wouldn't . . . 1250 for each
         half hour. Well, uh, thank you very much. Bye.
To Burns.
         He said he'll put it to them but he's almost certain
         it'll be, it'll be no . . . but I think he's going to
         come back with 2,000, I bet. For two shows.

BURNS   Then, then we're no better off. We're still better
         off the other way with one show. Aren't we, Albert?

GROSSMAN   I don't know.

BURNS   I don't, uh . . .

GROSSMAN   Can we, without, uh, acting in bad taste,
         can we get Johnny Hamp back on the, on the
         phone and, and tell him it looks like we have a
         better offer from, uh . . . I'll tell him. No?

BURNS   Albert, if I may, if you go along with me,
         'cause I know Johnny, and Johnny's a good guy—
         in other words, Johnny is not about to save them
         money, you know.

GROSSMAN   I know. We only asked for two. He's
      certainly not going to come with more than that.
      I mean, he's certainly not going to come back and say
      we'd like to give you a little more than you asked for.

BURNS   Well, what we can do is this. If you want to
      hold on, Johnny'll be back in the morning, and
      if he comes up with the two, and if they've turned
      'round in the end, and say, you know, "forget it,"
      we no go. If they come up with the two, I'll say
      "Look, Johnny, as your friend because Albert wants
      to do it with you, we're telling this to you, we're
      not saying no to you and doing the other one, we're
      going to tell you straight what happened. We
      were ready to do yours if you came up with the two
      but then the BBC got raving mad and came up
      with two. So you've got to top it."
On the telephone.
      Albert? Um, Albert, Stewart? I'll be with Albert
      in a few moments and
Holds up two fingers for Grossman . . . Grossman smiles.
      Um, I'll put it to him and uh, uh, and you know I'm
      sure he'll come up with a decision, you know,
      very quickly. Well now Stewart, let me tell you,
      between you and I, um . . . very truthfully, you know,
      oh, like two months ago, Granada came on when
      they heard he was coming, and, you know them,
      they pay . . . you know, what, they pay for the taxi
      as well, if you know what I mean. Uh, and they've
      been on there hammering away like mad. So, uh,
      Albert does have a pretty tough decision in a
      way. But, you've seen today's chart? Dylan: number
      six, "Subterranean Homesick Blues." Yeah, jumped
      from like 45 or something to six. Yeah, I'll be
      with Albert within ten minutes or so.
Albert looks up at Tito.

Newcastle

*Dylan stands in front of a guitar store window that is
filled with electric guitars. Sign on window
advertises "Subterranean Homesick Blues."*

DYLAN   Look at this guitar, man.

PENNEBAKER   Which one?

DYLAN   This one right there. Do you believe that guitar?
They don't have those guitars in the states, man.
They're incredible. Twenty grand?

Laughter.

In a back room Dylan plays piano and hums;
  Tom Wilson listens.
Outside concert hall.

GIRLS IN CROWD   *In heavy north country accent.*
  Here he comes!
Dylan appears and disappears almost instantly.
  I don't know. He had it cut down there.
Girl who is speaking combs hair forward with fingers.
  And long sideburns.

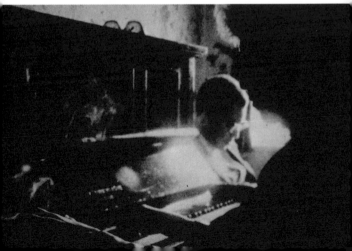

THE SCIENCE STUDENT

In dressing room, Dylan faces interviewers.

DYLAN   You think it would bother me one little bit
if you disliked me?

SCIENCE STUDENT   Um, no.

DYLAN   Or anybody disliked me?

SCIENCE STUDENT   No, no, but some people might
not like you.

DYLAN   No, no, you know, I got my friends, I mean.
I'm well situated.

SCIENCE STUDENT   What about before you had any
friends? Did you, um, were you worried then?

DYLAN   Was I worried? No, I wasn't worried about it, no.
I was lucky then. Weren't you?

SCIENCE STUDENT   I think I've got a few friends now.

DYLAN   Weren't your friends lucky when you didn't have
any friends?

SCIENCE STUDENT   I can't remember never having
any friends.

DYLAN   Huh? Do you have a lot of friends now?

SCIENCE STUDENT   No! Because, because, um . . . I
reached a stage when I suddenly realized what a
friend was, and then, I probably had one or two.
Before that, I probably didn't understand what
a friend was anyway.

DYLAN   Do you talk to your friends?

SCIENCE STUDENT   I didn't know who they were then.

DYLAN Well, now, now, your friends. Do you talk to your friends?

SCIENCE STUDENT Yeah, there are one or two people I believe I can talk to.

DYLAN That's why they're your friends because you can talk to them?

SCIENCE STUDENT Um, I think of a friend as a friend because . . .

DYLAN Can you communicate with them?

SCIENCE STUDENT To a certain extent. They can understand me more than anybody else.

DYLAN Oh, oh yeah, that's where we differ, we differ. We come from two different worlds. You come from England, I come from the United States.

SCIENCE STUDENT Yes, true. It's true but I . . . we're still human beings so there's some sort of, uh, connection between us.

DYLAN No, I'm just a guitar player. That's all.

SCIENCE STUDENT Man, you're trying to knock me.

DYLAN Uh, believe me, uh, I'm not trying to do that.

SCIENCE STUDENT Uh, I mean when somebody comes in to interview you, normally, what's your attitude?

DYLAN Oh, you just read those interviews that were . . . the first few days I was here.

SCIENCE STUDENT Um, uh, yeah, yeah . . .

DYLAN Um, those were not right, you know, you know, you know. I mean you know that, right, you know that that was all lies, lies, rubbish. You know that!
Alan plays blues riff on piano.

SCIENCE STUDENT   . . . The first few lines and then I didn't read much more. Why I came I don't know. I'm being regaled with all this. . . .

DYLAN   Are you going to the concert?

SCIENCE STUDENT   Yeah, I'm going to watch. I mean, I, I . . . well this is what I came to see mostly. . . .

DYLAN   Listen. . . .

SCIENCE STUDENT   I came to see you. . . .

DYLAN   Listen. . . .

SCIENCE STUDENT   But I thought I might have a word with you first. I mean, what is your whole attitude to life? I mean, when you meet somebody, what is your attitude towards them?

DYLAN   I don't like them.

SCIENCE STUDENT   I mean, I come in here. What's your attitude towards me?

DYLAN   No, I don't have an attitude towards you at all. Why should I have an attitude towards you? I don't even know you.

SCIENCE STUDENT   No, but I mean and it would be an attitude if you wanted to know me or didn't want to know me.

DYLAN Well, why should I want to know you?

SCIENCE STUDENT I don't know . . . that's what I'm asking.

DYLAN Well, I don't know. Ask me another question. Just give me a reason why I should want to know you.

SCIENCE STUDENT Um . . . I might be worth knowing.

DYLAN Why?

SCIENCE STUDENT Huh?

DYLAN Why? Tell me why. What good is it going to do me for me to know you? Tell me. Give me, name me one thing I'm going to gain.

SCIENCE STUDENT Well, you might learn something from my attitude to life.

DYLAN Well, what is your attitude towards life? Huh?

SCIENCE STUDENT I can't explain that in two minutes.

DYLAN Well, what are you asking me to explain in two minutes? . . .

SCIENCE STUDENT Huh? . . .

DYLAN . . . That's all you're getting is two minutes. You're asking me to explain something in two minutes too.

SCIENCE STUDENT But you're the artist. You're supposed to be able to explain it in two minutes.

DYLAN I am?

SCIENCE STUDENT Yeah.

DYLAN Hey, now, what about you? Aren't you an artist?

SCIENCE STUDENT Oh, no.

DYLAN What are you?

SCIENCE STUDENT I'm a science student.

DYLAN Well, let's hear it again, what are you? A what student?

SCIENCE STUDENT A science student.

DYLAN Now, what does that mean? Just what does that mean?

SCIENCE STUDENT Hmmmmm?

DYLAN What does that mean? What do you do? What's your purpose in the world?

SCIENCE STUDENT Ummm . . . what's my purpose?

DYLAN Yeah.

SCIENCE STUDENT What's my purpose in the world?

DYLAN Yeah. How do you help? You know. What do you do in the world?

SCIENCE STUDENT   Well, I'm uh, uh, uh, I'm in the
world for me, I guess.

DYLAN   Well . . .

SCIENCE STUDENT   Like everybody else.

DYLAN   Just like me.

SCIENCE STUDENT   Yeah, yeah.

DYLAN   So we're just alike, aren't we?

SCIENCE STUDENT   I guess so.

DYLAN   We don't come from two different worlds.

SCIENCE STUDENT   No, we're both alike.

DYLAN   We both come from, uh, Prussia.

SCIENCE STUDENT   You're wrong, you're wrong. I was
right, I was right—all the time. No, but this, I mean,
this is interesting. Now I go, I go to interview
to groups, if I go interview Alan's mob. I don't
think they're, they, they couldn't care less about me,
you know.

DYLAN Well, you know, why should, you know, haven't you ever stopped to wonder why?

SCIENCE STUDENT Ummmmmm.
Laughter.

DYLAN There's gotta be some reason, doesn't there? I mean it just doesn't happen.

SCIENCE STUDENT Yeah, yeah, but it's nothing to do with me because they don't wanna know me before I go in.

DYLAN Huh? Well, what do you want from them?

SCIENCE STUDENT Before I go, I don't know them, I don't . . .

DYLAN What do you want? Can you write them up in your paper? That's not it. What's that?

SCIENCE STUDENT No, I don't, I don't think of myself as . . . as . . . as. . . .

87

DYLAN   Are you going to give them to science?

SCIENCE STUDENT   I'm, I'm a person, you know.

DYLAN   Well, so what   there's a million, thousand,
     billion—there's so many persons outside.

SCIENCE STUDENT   Yeah, I agree, absolutely.

DYLAN   Only you can't know them all.

SCIENCE STUDENT   No, no but a . . . if I meet somebody,
     ah, speak to them a few minutes I think that guy
     might be able to give me something.

DYLAN   Well, ah . . . oh ho.
Everybody laughs.
     Now we're . . . now we're getting down there, huh.
     Yeah, what is it that you want?

SCIENCE STUDENT   Um, everyone is out for what
     they can get.

DYLAN   What is it?

SCIENCE STUDENT   Well, I might be able to get . . .
     I might be able to get something material.

DYLAN   You might be able to get a chick!

SCIENCE STUDENT   Huh?
Laughter.

DYLAN   You might be able to get a chick?
Laughter and joking.

NEUWIRTH   Here.
Hands him harp.

SCIENCE STUDENT   I don't want it, I don't want it,
     I can't play that thing.

NEUWIRTH   Now you got it.

DYLAN We don't want it either.

SCIENCE STUDENT Well, I can't play it.
Laughter.

SCIENCE STUDENT You know what I meant by give
something material. I'm not necessarily interested . . .

DYLAN What are they going to give you spiritually?
SCIENCE STUDENT Uh, I might learn something.

DYLAN What?

SCIENCE STUDENT Huh?

DYLAN What! What don't you know that you want
to know?

SCIENCE STUDENT OK.

ALAN PRICE You get a kick out of interviewing people,
ya know.

SCIENCE STUDENT Ohhh, come on, Alan, if I talked
to somebody. . . .

PRICE . . . People had better sense 'cause I don't know.
They ask the same questions 'cause nobody . . .
I mean . . . you got interviewers a million times
ask the same stupid thing so . . .

SCIENCE STUDENT Well, do interviewers ask the same
questions as me?

PRICE Yeah, obviously they do because . . .

SCIENCE STUDENT They do?
PRICE . . . You don't know what to ask anybody
because you don't know what's on any person's mind
anyway. Who wants to talk to anybody who doesn't...

SCIENCE STUDENT Well, I won't know if I don't try
to find out, will I?

PRICE   Not the way you try.

SCIENCE STUDENT   Huh?

DYLAN   Don'tcha, do you ever just be quiet? Be silent and just watch and don't say one word?

SCIENCE STUDENT   Yeah, the, the whole thing that gets me about, about you and about Alan is the fact that you're knocking from the minute I come in.

DYLAN   Knocking?

SCIENCE STUDENT   Yeah! You're not interested.

DYLAN   I don't think you know when you're liked, that's all. If we, you know, if we wanted to knock you we could put you on.

SCIENCE STUDENT   Yeah, but I mean he just said that I'm talking a lot of rubbish, you know and a . . .

PRICE   I never said that. You're misquoting me already. You see, that's another journalistic trick. . . .

SCIENCE STUDENT   Ah . . . no I didn't misquote you, I interpreted you.

DYLAN   Interpreted him to your own thing, right? To your own rules of . . . ah, your own images.

SCIENCE STUDENT   I have to give some answer.

GROSSMAN   Why?
Laughter.

SCIENCE STUDENT   Huh?

GROSSMAN   Why do you have to give some answer?

SCIENCE STUDENT   Well, to satisfy you.

GROSSMAN   You don't have to satisfy me. The only thing . . .

NEUWIRTH   Besides, it's impossible.
Laughter.

SCIENCE STUDENT   If you had said you didn't want an answer I wouldn't have given one.

DYLAN   Do you always try to satisfy everybody?

SCIENCE STUDENT   No.

DYLAN   Do you every once in a while try?

SCIENCE STUDENT   Hmmm?

DYLAN   Do you every once in a while try to satisfy somebody?

SCIENCE STUDENT   Somebody, yeah, not everybody.

DYLAN   Yeah, a few people though, uh?

SCIENCE STUDENT   Well, some people I can't satisfy because that's the way I'm made.

DYLAN   Yeah.

SCIENCE STUDENT   No matter how hard I try I couldn't satisfy them.

DYLAN   Well, how do you know that?

SCIENCE STUDENT   Hmmmmm?

DYLAN   How do you know that?

SCIENCE STUDENT   Well, after you get to know somebody for a little while you can guess just uhmmm. . . .

DYLAN   Are you still friends with them even though you can't satisfy them?

SCIENCE STUDENT   Yeah, friends, not deep friends, not deep friends. You find it's the . . .

DYLAN   What's a deep friend?

SCIENCE STUDENT   Well, it's somebody that you're almost exactly on the same plane with them.

DYLAN   So it means you're just like them.

SCIENCE STUDENT   You can communicate with them very well.

DYLAN   Somebody that they're just like you.

SCIENCE STUDENT   Uh . . . not exa . . .

DYLAN   Looks like you.

SCIENCE STUDENT   No.

DYLAN   No?

SCIENCE STUDENT   No.

DYLAN   Talks like you?

SCIENCE STUDENT   Uhmmmm.

DYLAN   Well, how do you mean like somebody?

SCIENCE STUDENT   Thinks the same way.

DYLAN   Thinks the same way?

SCIENCE STUDENT   Thinks the same way.

DYLAN   Like what? Like we both think that, uh, that we want, that, uh, that both are happy about a green door?

SCIENCE STUDENT   No, think in the same language.

DYLAN   Think in the same language.

SCIENCE STUDENT   Yeah.

DYLAN   Uh huh.

SCIENCE STUDENT   And so you can understand each other. And you know what each other are thinking.

DYLAN   Well, let's try and understand each other, shall we?

SCIENCE STUDENT   That wouldn't be a bad idea. That wouldn't be a bad idea. And how are we going to set about . . .

DYLAN   Well, you can ask your first question.

SCIENCE STUDENT   Hmmmm?

DYLAN   You can ask your first question.

SCIENCE STUDENT   Ah . . .

DYLAN   Go ahead. You got a question to ask? Come on.

SCIENCE STUDENT   Ah . . .

DYLAN   You haven't got any questions?

SCIENCE STUDENT   Well, I didn't.
Knock on door.

DYLAN   I think somebody's calling for you.

SCIENCE STUDENT   You want me to go.

NEUWIRTH   I'll get it.
Goes to door and looks outside.

DYLAN   No, you don't have to go.

SCIENCE STUDENT   No, I didn't come in here, I mean,
    I don't consider myself, I mean, he considers me
    a journalist. I'm not a journalist.

NEUWIRTH   Hey, man, the high sheriff's lady would
    like to talk to you.

DYLAN   Who is the high sheriff's lady?
Laughter.

NEUWIRTH   Ho, ho, would I know? Ha, ha, do I look
    like Robin Hood? Who the hell's the high sheriff, man?

GROSSMAN   It's Sarah Lee.
Laughter.
    She's thirteen years old.

DYLAN   Where is this high sheriff's lady?
Looks cautiously out door.

NEUWIRTH   I think she's a big cheese. She's next door.

94

VOICE   Mrs. Jim Clark.

PRICE   Mrs. Jim Clark . . .
Laughs.

NEUWIRTH   Jim Clark is the sheriff of Nottingham.
Continued crowd noise and laughter.

NEUWIRTH   She wants to say hello.

DYLAN   *sits on piano keyboard with slight musical effect.*
   Who is she?

NEUWIRTH   I don't know. The guard just told me.
   The high sheriff's lady . . . I just thought you might
   get knocked out by the high sheriff's lady
   wanting to see you.
Laughs.

The High Sheriff's Lady

HIGH SHERIFF'S LADY I'm the sheriff's lady. And I'm
to say on behalf of all of them I've come to say,
how very happy we are to have you here. And
we hope you have a very successful night because
everybody loves you. There are thousands outside.
And these are my three boys—David, Steven
and Steven—and they think you're so marvelous
that they've left all their exam papers. They've got
terribly important exams and they've left
everything to come and listen to you.

DYLAN *smiles nervously.*
Oh, okay.

LADY So that I do think you'd better be good. Oh,
you are good. I don't think you can help being good.
But we're really very thrilled indeed to have you
here. And if you come after May again, then I'll have
you as my guest in the mansion house.

MAN   This lady will be Lord Mayor after May. . . .

DYLAN   After May. . . .

LADY   After May—when you come back. You see, I
think the songs are very wonderful.

DYLAN   Thank you.

LADY   And you write them yourself, too, don't you
sometimes?

DYLAN   I write them all, yeah.

LADY   Yes, have you really? Yes, because they've got
feeling and they're really marvelous. And I really
mean this, I think you're really a good example
for the youth.

DYLAN   Thank you.

LADY   So that if you come back again, I shall be
delighted to have you both as my guests in the
mansion house.

DYLAN   Oh, here he is, my friend.

NEUWIRTH   This uh, we have something for you too.

LADY   How do you do, how do you do.

NEUWIRTH   Oh yeah, would you like that?
Hands her harp.

LADY   Ooohh, love it! Is it from you?
Turns to Dylan.

DYLAN   Yeah, it's mine. If you use one that's a new one,
that's an old one.

LADY   Thank you very much indeed! That's very lovely
of you. Now, if you're his friend I've just invited your
friend if he comes any time after May to come
with his manager and you and stay in my
mansion house.

NEUWIRTH   Groovy! . . . groovy!

LADY   It's a beautiful place! Really, I mean this.

LADY   I shall be Lord Mayor after May, God willing,
of this lovely city. And I really mean it. And I want
everyone to know what a wonderful city this is
and what hospitality we give. And also want you to
know how very thrilled we are to have you.
Thank you very much, goodbye, goodbye . . .
why, he's charming.

I Don't Feel Like Singing...

NEUWIRTH   It's 7:30 now?
    Oh shit.

DYLAN   Is it going to be late?

PRICE   *Stands at piano,
    playing and singing
    "Leaning on a Lamppost."*

DYLAN   What song is that?

GIRL   George Foley.

PRICE   He's the one who does
    "Mrs. Brown, You've Got a
    Lovely Daughter."

DYLAN   I heard it by Herman
    and the Hermits.
Laughter.

PRICE   *Sings a line of
    "Little Things."*
    We see that on television.
    Dave Berry, he does all
    these slow actions, man,
    he's like this, the human
    sloth, he does.
*Starts singing again and does
    elaborate imitation. Then
    plays piano and sings
    more of song.*

DYLAN   Hey, what do The Animals do for a piano
player now?

PRICE   They've got one since June. There's a good friend
of mine gonna go in later on for good, you know.

DYLAN   Aren't you playing with them no more?

PRICE   No, you know how it is. That's the way it is,
it just happens, you know.
*Makes wry face. Dylan starts to play blues on his guitar—
Price turns to piano, plays. Sings several
disconnected blues phrases.*

DYLAN   Oh man, I don't feel like singing.

NEUWIRTH   You will when you get out there. Two
encores or one, man?

DYLAN   Maybe one. I don't know, you know, maybe . . .
why don't we just make it one?
Goes out door with Neuwirth and others.

PRICE   Who did I give the matches to before? I gotta
open this somewhere. Have you got an opener here?
Neuwirth peeks in door, Price opens beer bottle on piano.

NEUWIRTH   Taking a bottle of sauce to work? Did you
get glass in that?

PRICE   No, wood.
Laughs. They go out and close door.

PART 2

Don't Think Twice...

DYLAN *sings on stage—Newcastle.*
And it ain't no use in callin' out my name, Babe
Like you never did before
And it ain't no use in callin' out my name, Babe
I can't hear you anymore.
I'm thinkin' and a wonderin' walkin'
all the way down the road
I once loved a woman, a child I'm told
I gave her my heart but she wanted my soul
But don't think twice, it's all right.

As he finishes verse and plays harp chorus he is
suddenly on train traveling across English landscape.
Neat row houses. Finally, bare countryside. Dylan
puts hands over eyes. Train arrives in Manchester.

MANCHESTER

On stage in empty hall.

DYLAN   *rehearsing mike levels.*
  What about that? What?

NEUWIRTH   Keep playing.

DYLAN   What are you doing?

NEUWIRTH   Look, I want to find out where the sound
  system goes.

DYLAN   Where are you? The last time I talked to you
  you were over here.

NEUWIRTH   Look, do you want to keep it like that?

DYLAN   Are you heading over this way now?

NEUWIRTH   Yeah.

DYLAN   All right.
Cuts to escape. After concert, running down stairs.

DYLAN   Where's the door?

NEUWIRTH   Down the stairs. Follow the stairs.

DYLAN   Where man?
*In background "God Save The Queen" announces the
        end of the concert. Dylan has until its completion
        to escape.*

NEUWIRTH   Come on, let's go.

VOICE   Down the stairs, down the stairs.
*They run down endless halls and turn, end of "Queen"
        approaches ominously.*
They finally emerge into street filled with screaming fans.

VOICE IN NIGHT   Get a taxi, Pete, come on! Pete,
        get a taxi. Quick!
Girls squeal and scream.

WHO THREW THE GLASS IN THE STREET...

Dylan's hotel room—party—Donovan listens, as one of his records plays in background.

DYLAN *from other side of room, breaks in suddenly.*
Hey come on, I want to know who threw that glass in the street? Who did it? Now, you better tell me, now if somebody doesn't tell me who did it, you all gonna get the fuck outa here and never come back. Now, who did it? I don't care who did it, man, I just wanna know who did it.

DRUNK   I'm pissed . . . I was out there in the bathroom,
        coming out . . .

DYLAN   Hey, don't tell me you're pissed, man. Don't
        tell me you're pissed because I don't want to
        hear you're pissed.

DRUNK   I'm not, I'm not.

DYLAN   Who threw the glass in the street?

DRUNK   I didn't throw the glass.

DYLAN Well, who did it? Tell me, you were there—
who threw it? You know who?

FRIEND OF DRUNK Yeah, I know who, Bob. But
you know . . .

DYLAN All right, hey, I don't care who did it. If you
know who did it you just better tell whoever did it
to get out there and tell the cats that come up
here to ask who did it, tell them who it was. I'm not
taking no fucking responsibility for cats I don't
know, man. I got enough responsibility with my
friends and my own people.

DRUNK I, I agree.

DYLAN Now, now come on!

DRUNK I was out there . . .

DYLAN I don't care who was . . .

DRUNK . . . When you asked who did it.

DYLAN I don't want no—none of your—none of
your shit man.

DRUNK I'm not givin' you shit.

DYLAN Throwing a glass in the street!

DRUNK I'm not givin' you shit.

DYLAN What'd you do it for man? What'd you do it
for, I mean, what'd you throw a glass in the street for?

DRUNK I didn't throw a glass in the street.

DYLAN Well, show me the person that did it. If you
don't have him here by the time I count to ten
you better take the responsibility for him.

DRUNK All right.

DYLAN All right—one, two, three, four, five, six, seven, eight, nine, ten . . . you got him here?

DRUNK No.

DYLAN Hey, man, I'm not kidding. You think I'm kidding. He's gonna clean up that glass, man, or I'll clean it up.

VOICE I'll clean up your glass, man.

DONOVAN Hey, I'll help you man.

DRUNK I wouldn't clean your . . .

DARROLL ADAMS He's all right . . . he's . . .

DYLAN Hey, I believe he's all right, man. I believe he's all right. Well, okay, I believe it.

DRUNK Listen . . .

DYLAN I know a thousand cats that look just like you, man, talk just like you.

DRUNK Ah, fuck off. You're a big noise, you know.

DYLAN I know it man, I know I'm a big noise. I'm a bigger noise than you, man.

DRUNK I'm a small noise.

DYLAN Right.

DRUNK I'm a small cat.

DYLAN That's right.

DRUNK If I'd thrown a fucking glass in the street . . .

DYLAN *Shoves him.*

  You're anything you say you are, man.

DRUNK I'm nothing!

DYLAN   You say you're small
     . . . you're nothing.

DRUNK   I'm nothing!

DYLAN   I believe you.

DRUNK   Nothing.

DYLAN   I believe you, man.

DERROLL ADAMS   Boys.

DRUNK   Listen, you're Bobby
     Dylan, aren't you. You're a
     big noise.

ADAMS   You know, couldn't we
     have a drink over here?

DRUNK   You're a big
     international noise, you
     know?

ADAMS   Boys . . .

DYLAN   Right . . .

DRUNK   I'm nothing . . .

DYLAN   Right . . .

DRUNK   I didn't throw any
     fucking glass in the street,
     man. You know, if I had . . .

ADAMS   Yeah, that's true.

DRUNK   And I wanted to believe it . . .

DYLAN   Well, who did man?

DRUNK   You know, and if you'd a wanted to, you know, come at me for your fucking glasses . . .

VOICE   Yeah, that's true.

DRUNK   You know, you know . . . I'd a had to go at you.

DYLAN   All right . . .

DRUNK   All these guys, all these guys . . .

DYLAN   Okay.

DRUNK   So I'm going, you know . . .

DYLAN   Okay.

DRUNK   So I didn't . . .

DYLAN   Okay.

DRUNK   So, you know, the cats'll see . . .

DYLAN   Hey, just tell the cat that, that we're coming down to sweep it up. That's all you have to say to him. Just tell the cat we're coming down to sweep it up.

DRUNK   I'll go down. I will go down to sweep it up.

DYLAN   No, you don't have to. Just tell him we'll come down and do it.

VOICE   Be groovy, right, right?

DYLAN   Yeah, either be groovy or leave man. You don't have to be groovy for me. Just be groovy for anybody who you want to be groovy for.

NEUWIRTH   There's a gentleman here inquiring about a glass.

HOWARD ALK   Just tell me who you want to stay, man.

DYLAN   Right . . . a lot of people can stay, man. Oh man.

WAITER   It hit a car . . . we've got trouble, you see.

DYLAN   Uh, okay. We'll find out who did it. Ah, we won't find out who did it. Hey, I'm sorry about that.
Later . . .

DYLAN *to Derroll Adams.*
> You used to wear a cowboy hat like Jack, right?
> I got a record of yours and Jack's. I have one called
> "The Cowboys" . . . "The Cowboys" and also, ah . . .

DERROLL ADAMS Ramblin' Boys.

DYLAN Ramblin Boys? The Ramblin' Boys and
> The Cowboys.

ADAMS Yeah.

DYLAN *leans over and takes drunk's hand.*
> I just didn't want any, I didn't want that glass . . .
> if you're sober, I didn't want that glass to hurt
> anybody.

DRUNK What?

DYLAN I just didn't want that glass to hurt anybody.

DRUNK It didn't.

DYLAN Okay.

ADAMS Listen man, why don't we get together and
> I'll turn you on to some things.

DYLAN *sitting on floor.*
> Okay. Are there any poets like Allan Ginsberg
> around, man?

ADAMS No, no, nothing like that—Dominic Behan.

DYLAN Hey, yeah, yeah, you know, you know.
> No, I don't wanna hear nobody like Dominic Behan,
> man, Dominic Behan.

DRUNK Dominic Behan is a friend of mine.

DYLAN Hey, that's fine, man. I just don't wanta hear
> anybody like that though.
Donovan begins playing guitar.
> Hey, he plays like Jack, man.

DONOVAN

DONOVAN *sings a verse of "To Sing for You."*

DYLAN Hey, that's a good song, man.

DONOVAN *sings next verse. Applause.*

DYLAN That's okay, man.

VOICE Hey, play one, Bob, play one.

DONOVAN I wanna hear "It's All Over Now, Baby Blue."

DYLAN You wanna hear that song? Do you have a flat pick?

DONOVAN I got that in "D" tuning.

DYLAN What key did you tune it down to?

DONOVAN "D" tuning.

DYLAN *sings.*
> You must leave, take what you need
> You think will last
> But whatever you wish to keep
> You'd better grab it fast.
> Yonder stands your orphan with his gun
> Crying like a fire in the sun
> Look out, the saints are coming through
> And it's all over now, baby blue.
>
> The highway is for gamblers,
> Better use your sense.
> Take what you have gathered from coincidence
> The vagabond, he's rapping at your door
> He's standing in the clothes
> That you once wore.
> Strike another match,
> Go start anew.
> And it's all over now, baby blue.

DONOVAN Great, Bob.

VOICE That's nice, Bob.

DONOVAN *Softly, to himself.*
> I used to know a girl named Baby Blue.

DYLAN Do you wanna hear another song?

Next day in hotel room.

FRED   *on phone.*
    Is that the stage door?

DYLAN   *in background.*
    What was that?

Talks to Allan Ginsberg.

FRED   *on phone.*
    Please, yes, this is the
    Savoy Hotel. We're on our
    way in about ten minutes
    with Mr. Bob Dylan, so
    you shall expect us
    with . . . ? Through the
    stage door, there's not
    many kids there? Okay—
    right. Thanks very much.
    Bye.

To those in room.
    There's very few there
    apparently so . . .

ALL TICKETS
FOR SEATS AND
STANDING ROOM
ARE SOLD OUT
FOR BOB DYLAN
TO-NIGHT and TOMORROW

Sign at Royal Albert Hall reads . . .
"All tickets for seats and standing room for
Dylan concert sold out."

Neuwirth, Dylan, Fred in cab on way to hall.

NEUWIRTH Beautiful day, man.

FRED Been in the office all day, since 10 o'clock
in the morning.

NEUWIRTH Really?

FRED Organizing my other tour.
Laughs.

NEUWIRTH The other folk singer?

FRED Donovan, yeah, the other folk singer.
Takes out cigarette.

DYLAN How's that tour doing?

FRED Uh, not so good.
Neuwirth laughs.

FRED He says to me, what do you think if I book a
theatre in Scarborough for a Sunday concert and
put, um, just Donovan all on his own? I said, well,
you know, I can't see it for two hours, you know.

FRED He said, do you think we should book one
other act? I said we should book about four other acts.
Laughs.

DYLAN *lights cigarette and turns to window,
saying nothing.*

Royal Albert Hall

DYLAN *In dark, at back of theatre.*
  Wow, this must be a very old theatre, huh?

GIRL Sure, Victoria died 1804.

NEUWIRTH Queen Victoria built it for her dude.

DYLAN Look at it up there, man.

*Dylan and Neuwirth walk on
stage, approach seated girl.*

NEUWIRTH   This girl is the only
touch of reality. Look at all
the boxes . . .that is wild . . .
God!

DYLAN   Hello.
Echoes "hello."
*Outside—girl looks at program.
Crowd gathers.*

POLICEMAN   All over the place.

*Dressing room—Dylan slaps harp
on hand. Looks annoyed.*

DYLAN   Hey, I'll use it, man,
you know, I'll use it.

NEUWIRTH   Hey man, let's try
to get it straight!

GROSSMAN   We can always
pick up a new one.

NEUWIRTH   Lemme just try to
run some warm water
through it.

STAGE MANAGER   Are you
finished rehearsing now . . .
finished rehearsing?

GROSSMAN   Rehearsing,
finished with the stage, right?

STAGE MANAGER   Right.

DYLAN   *At piano with harmonica.*
I'll use it, you know, it's
passable. It's just, you
know, it's just a drag that
there's no new one.
*Grossman indicates without
speaking, "Wanna eat?"*

121

THE
INTERVIEW

Deserted lunch room at concert hall.

DYLAN   Are you going to see the concert tonight?

INTERVIEWER   Yes.

DYLAN   Are you going to hear it?

INTERVIEWER   Yes.

DYLAN Okay, you hear and see it and it's going to
        happen fast. Now, you're not going to get it all,
        and you might hear the wrong words, and then
        afterwards, see I can't . . . I won't be able to talk to
        you afterwards. I got nothing to say about these
        things I write, I mean, I just write them. I got nothing
        to say anything about them, I don't write 'em for
        any reason. There's no great message. I mean, if,
        you know, if you wanna tell other people that,
        you know, go ahead and tell them but I'm not going
        to have to answer to it. And, they're just going to
        think, you know, what's this *Time* Magazine telling us?
        But that, you couldn't care less about that either.
        You don't know the people that read you.

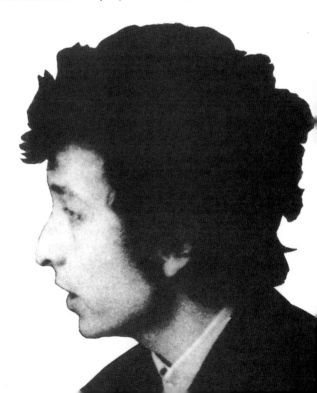

INTERVIEWER   Ah . . .

DYLAN   'Cause you know, I've never been in *Time*
Magazine and yet this hall's filled twice, you know,
and I've never been in *Time* Magazine. I don't need
Time Magazine . . . and I don't think I'm a folk singer.
You'll probably call me a folk singer but, you know,
the other people know better 'cause the people,
you know, that buy my records, listen to me, don't
necessarily read *Time* Magazine. You know, the
audience that subscribe to *Time* Magazine? The
audience of the people that want to know what's
happening in the world week by week. The people
that work during the day and can read it small, right?
And it's concise, and there's pictures in it.

I mean, those kind of, you know, those . . . a
certain class of people. It's a class of people that take
the magazine seriously. I mean, sure I could read it,
you know, I read it. I read it on the airplanes
but I don't take it seriously. If I want to find out
anything I'm not going to read *Time* Magazine.
I'm not gonna read *Newsweek*. I'm not gonna read
any of these magazines, I mean, 'cause they just
got too much to lose by printing the truth,
you know that.

INTERVIEWER   What kind of truths do they leave out?

DYLAN   On anything! Even on a worldwide basis.
They'd just go off the stands in a day if they printed
really the truth.

INTERVIEWER   What is really the truth?

DYLAN   Really the truth is just a plain picture.

INTERVIEWER   Of what? Particularly.

DYLAN   Of, you know, a plain picture of, let's say,
a tramp vomiting, man, into the sewer. You know,
and next door to the picture, you know,
Mr. Rockefeller, you know, or Mr. C. W. Jones,
you know, on the subway going to work, you know,
any kind of picture. Just make some sort of collage
of pictures which they don't do. They don't do.
There's no ideas in *Time* Magazine, there's just these
facts. Well, you know, which too are switched
because even the article which you are doing, the
way it's gonna come out, don't you see, it can't
be a good article. Because, the guy that's writing the
article is sitting in a desk in New York, he's not,
he is not even going out of his office. He's just going
to get, all these, ah, 15, you know, reporters and
they're gonna send him a quota, you know.

INTERVIEWER   That's not me . . .

DYLAN   No, he's going to put himself on, he's going to
put all his readers on, and you know, in another
week we have some space in the magazine. But that's
all, it means nothing to anybody else. I'm not putting
that down because people have gotta eat and live,
you know, but let's at least be honest about it.
You know, I mean sure, let's say, let's say . . .

INTERVIEWER   I just don't, I don't know that you
are giving me . . .

DYLAN   I know more about what you do and you don't
even have to ask me how or why or anything,
just by looking, you know, than you'll ever know

about me, ever. I mean, I could tell you, I could tell you I'm not a folk singer and explain to you why, but you wouldn't really understand. All you could do, you could nod your head, you would nod your head.

INTERVIEWER   You could be willing to try, and . . .

DYLAN   No, I couldn't even be willing to try because, it is, you know, it would be, it's, you know, there're certain things which . . . every word, every word has its little letter and big letter.

INTERVIEWER   Your friend had the right word— pigeonhole.

NEUWIRTH   No, no, it's not important . . .

DYLAN   No, it's not pigeonhole, it's not the word at all. You know, every word has its little letter and big letter, like the word "know."

INTERVIEWER   Yeah.

DYLAN   You know, the word know, "k-n-o-w?"

INTERVIEWER   Yeah.

DYLAN   Okay, then you know the word know, capital "K-N-O-W?"

INTERVIEWER   Yeah.

DYLAN   Like, each of us really "knows" nothing.

INTERVIEWER   Yeah.

DYLAN   Right? But we all think we know things.

INTERVIEWER   Right.

DYLAN   And, we really know nothing.

INTERVIEWER   But you're saying you know more about what I do . . .

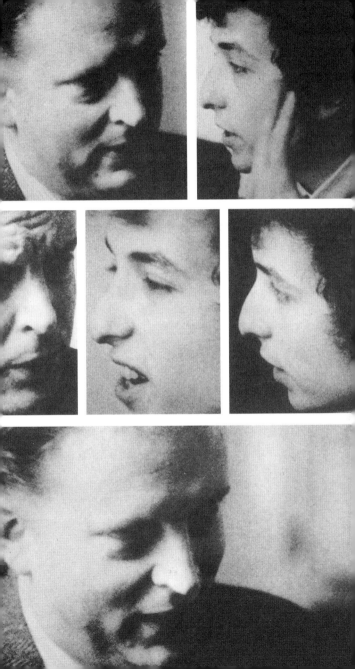

DYLAN   No, I'm saying, I'm saying, I'm saying . . .

NEUWIRTH   No, no, no.

DYLAN   I'm saying that you're going to die, and you're
        gonna go off the earth, you're gonna be dead.
        Man, it could be, you know, twenty years, it could be
        tomorrow, any time, so am I. I mean, we're just
        gonna be gone. The world's going to go on without us.

INTERVIEWER   Right.

DYLAN   All right now, you do your job in the face of
        that and how seriously you take yourself, you
        decide for yourself.

INTERVIEWER   Right.

DYLAN   Okay, now I'll decide for myself. Now, you're
        not going to make me feel unhappy by anything you
        print about me or anything, you know, or anything
        like that. It's just, it couldn't, you know, you couldn't
        offend me. And, I'm sure you know I couldn't
        offend you. And so all I can hope for you to do is,
        uh, all your ideas in your own head, somehow,
        wherever they are . . .

INTERVIEWER   Do you care about what you sing?

DYLAN   How could I answer that if you've got the
        nerve to ask me?

INTERVIEWER   Well then you, how could you . . .

DYLAN   I mean, you've got a lot of nerve asking me
        a question like that.

INTERVIEWER   I have to ask that.

DYLAN   Do you ask The Beatles that?

INTERVIEWER   I have to ask you that because you have
        the nerve to question whether I can . . .

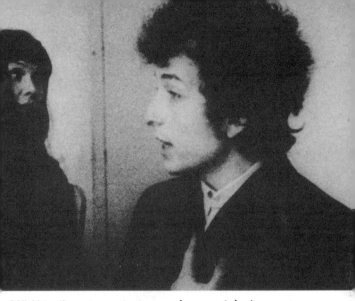

DYLAN   I'm not questioning you because I don't expect
         any answer from you. Do you think somebody
         wouldn't go see somebody if they didn't want
         entertainment?

INTERVIEWER   Of course not.

DYLAN   Who, now who wants to go get whipped,
         you know, and if you do wanna go get whipped,
         hey, aren't you really being entertained?

INTERVIEWER   All right . . . So fine.

DYLAN   Right.

INTERVIEWER   It's all right.

DYLAN   Okay. So, if you think anybody that comes to
         see me is coming for any other reason except
         entertainment, really.

INTERVIEWER   They'll tell you they're all coming for
         different reasons.

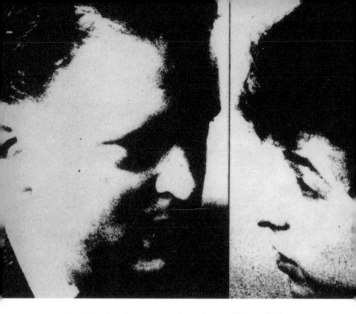

DYLAN Well, who cares what they tell you. Who cares what anybody tells you.

INTERVIEWER Well, they think they, they think they know why they're doing it.

DYLAN Well, do you know why they're doing it?

INTERVIEWER I know some of the things they say. . . .

DYLAN People say all kinds of things. . . .

INTERVIEWER Uh hummm.

DYLAN And you have to sort of . . . to weed it out. Can you weed it out?

INTERVIEWER Well, that's what I'm trying to do.

DYLAN Yeah, well, you see, you have to learn but I can't teach you how to weed it out.

INTERVIEWER Yeah, I didn't say that I couldn't do that, I said I don't mean that.

DYLAN   Yeah, well you know, I have no idea. First of all, I'm not even a pop singer.

INTERVIEWER   You think you have a big audience?

DYLAN   I don't know. I have no idea.

INTERVIEWER   Well, you appeal to your audiences in some sense as a pop singer. Well, you know, even if it's Caruso he's, uh, you know, appealing to a popular, you know, this is a . . .

DYLAN   But, he's a pop singer . . . and I'm just as good a singer as Caruso. . . . Have you heard me sing? Have you ever heard me sing?

INTERVIEWER   I like Caruso better.

DYLAN   Ohhh . . . well, you see right there now, right there we have a little disagreement. I happen to be just as good as him . . . (laughter) a good singer, have to listen closely . . . (laughter) but I hit all those notes and I can hold my breath three times as long if I want to.

The Last Concert

*Ancient doorman opens doors of concert hall
and crowd surges in.*

DYLAN   *In dressing room, looks at clock. It is 7:20 pm.*
Is it going to start on time? Is it going to start on
time? Anybody say anything different?

VOICE   Do you know what time it's supposed to start?
7 o'clock?

DYLAN   7:30.

VOICE   7:30.

NEUWIRTH   I'd say ten minutes late.

DYLAN Donovan out there yet?

NEUWIRTH Hey, I can't see him . . . People like
Donovan . . . they look just like ordinary . . .
everybody . . . out there.

Out on street.

MAN Well anyway, all the seats are sold anyway.
Crowd noises.

Back inside.

GROSSMAN Are you getting all upset or not?

GIRL Yes, I am.

GROSSMAN Well, would you go someplace . . .
would you . . .

NEUWIRTH Hey, The Beatles are here.

VOICE They want to see him.
People continue to pour into hall.

DYLAN *Alone in dressing room with Grossman, bites lip.*
This sure'd be a lousy place, man, not to be able
to hear myself.

GROSSMAN You can hear yourself. Hey man, standing
right in back of you, you can hear yourself, right?
Ken Hyman knows. . . .

DYLAN Can I?

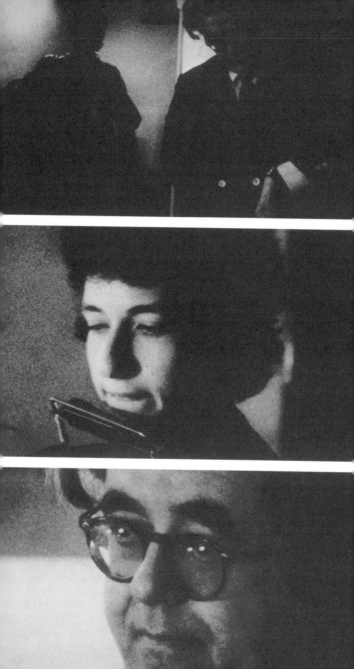

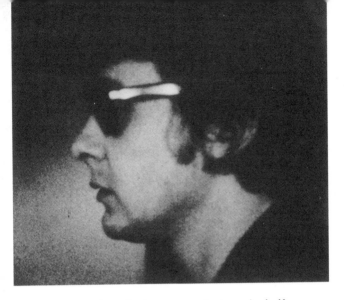

NEUWIRTH   About 2 minutes . . . minute and a half . . .
    next time I come in, it'll be time to go, so be ready.
Neuwirth goes out. Dylan gets ready. Neuwirth re-enters.

NEUWIRTH   Get your harps . . . come on, the hall's
    dark, man . . . let's go man.

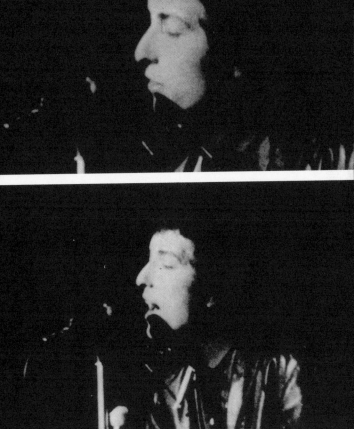

DYLAN   Hall all dark?

Walks onto stage, as in start of film, this time we follow
      him. Applause. Dylan sings:
      Come gather 'round people wherever you roam
      And admit that the waters around you have grown
      And accept it that soon you'll be drenched to the bone
      If your time to you is worth saving
      Then you'd better start swimming or you'll
            sink like a stone
      For the times they are a-changing.

139

Dissolves to:

> One time a crazy dream came to me,
> I dreamt I was walking in World War III.
> I went to the doctor the very next day
> To see what kind of things he had to say,
> He said it was a terrible dream

Audience laughs.

> I looked in the closet, there was Donovan

Audience laughs.

> Some of the people can be half right part of the time
> All of the people can be part right some of the time

Hesitates and audience laughs.

> Half of the people can be part right all of the time
> But all of the people can't be all right all of the time

Laughs.

> T. S. Eliot said that.

Dylan smiles and audience laughs.

> I'll let you be in my dream if I can be in your dream.
> I said that.

Applause.

This is called:
"It's All Right, Ma, I'm Only Bleeding, Ho, Ho, Ho."

Laughs—as he starts to play smile fades, music grows serious.

Darkness at the break of noon
Shadows even the silver spoon
The handmade blade, the child's balloon
Eclipses both the sun and moon
To understand, you know, too soon
There is no sense in trying.
As pointed threats they bluff with scorn
The suicide remarks are torn
From the fool's gold mouthpiece
The hollow horn plays wasted words
Proves to warn
That he not busy being born
Is busy dying.

Temptation's page flies out the door
You follow, find yourself at war
Watch waterfalls of pity roar
You feel to moan but unlike before
You discover that you'll just be
One more person crying.
So don't fear if you hear
A foreign sound in your ear
It's all right, Ma, I'm only sighing.

Dissolves to:

Of war and peace the truth just twists
Its curfew gull just glides
Upon four-legged forest clouds the cowboy angel rides.
With his candle cradled into the sun
Though its glow is waxed in black
All except when 'neath the trees of Eden.

The lamppost stands with folded arms
Its iron claws attached
To curbs 'neath holes where babies wail

Though it shadows metal badge
All in all can only fall
With a crashing but meaningless blow
And no sound at all ever comes from the gates of Eden.

The savage soldier sticks his head in sand
And then complains
Unto the shoeless hunter who's gone deaf
But still remains
Upon the beach where hound dogs bay
At ships with tattooed sails . . .

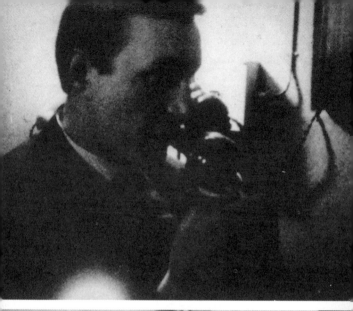

FRED *backstage, talks on house phone.*
   Limes out, house lights and the "Queen."
   Okay? Fair enough.

DYLAN *in dressing room.*
   Actually, applause is kind of bullshit.
Laughs.

NEUWIRTH Wouldn't that be something else, though,
   if they just sat there and waited?

DYLAN   *on stage, sings.*

> In the dime stores and bus stations
> People talk over situations
> Read books and repeat quotations
> Draw conclusions on the wall
> Some speak of the future
> My love she speaks softly
> She knows there's no success like failure
> And that failure's no success at all.
>
> The bridge at midnight trembles
> The country doctor rambles
> Bankers' nieces seek perfection
> Expecting all the gifts that wise men bring
> The wind howls like a hammer
> The night blows cold an' rainy
> My love she's like some raven
> At my window with a broken wing.

Applause.

After concert, getting into car.

NEUWIRTH   Go driver, go . . . go driver.

VOICE   Ah, beautiful.

NEUWIRTH   That was a good concert.

DYLAN   Huh?

NEUWIRTH   That was a good concert. Beautiful. They
were all there, man, all of them. God damn.
The vanishing American.

DYLAN   God, I feel like I've been through some kind
of . . . thing, man.

PENNEBAKER   *laughs.*
You have . . .

DYLAN   No, but I mean there was, something was,
something was special about it, that's all.

GROSSMAN   They've started calling you an anarchist.

DYLAN   Who?

GROSSMAN   The papers. That's the word now.
Laughter.

DYLAN   Anarchist. You're kidding. What papers did
you see that in?

GROSSMAN   Well, two or three. Today, yeah. Just 'caus
you don't offer any solution.

DYLAN   You're kidding!

GROSSMAN   Of course.

DYLAN   Anarchist.

GROSSMAN   Yeah.

DYLAN   Hmmmm. Gimme a cigarette. Give the
anarchist a cigarette.

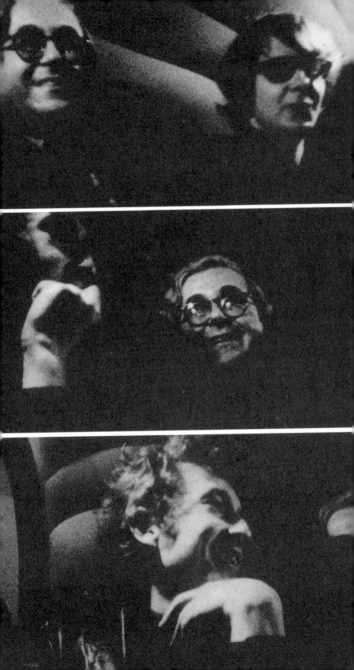

Laughter.

Anarchist, ohhh. A singer such as I!
Laughing.

GROSSMAN   Yeah, I was a little surprised to see it
   myself but . . .

GIRL   At least they didn't say communist.

DYLAN   But it probably took them a while to think of
   that name . . . anarchist. They couldn't say communist.

GIRL   Well, didn't they say that yesterday?

VOICE   Communists aren't in disfavor here.

DYLAN   Communists, you know, in England communists
   aren't really, ya know . . .

GIRL   Oh—it's cool to be . . .

DYLAN   Yeah . . .

VOICE   Cool to be . . .

DYLAN   I don't think it's cool to be an anarchist though.
Laughter.

GIRL   No, I'm sure it isn't . . .

DYLAN   Wherever it's at, man, I don't think it is.
*Laughter—Dylan turns and looks out window as car
   speeds through London.*

GROSSMAN   *very quietly sings.*
   It's all over now, baby blue.

The film
Produced by
Albert Grossman,
John Cort
and
Leacock Pennebaker Inc.

I would really like to thank Jones and Howard Alk who helped make it work, Bob Van Dyke who recorded the concerts, John Cooke who put the book togethet, Albert Grossman who gave it all a sense of purpose and, of course, all the participants who shall be nameless.

D. A. Pennebaker

ENDLESSLY FASCINATING...DONT LOOK BACK **is really** about fame and how it menaces art, about the press and how it categorizes, bowdlerizes, sterilizes, universalizes or conventionalizes an original like Dylan into something it can dimly understand. *NEWSWEEK*

SHOULD BE BURIED . . . This is a cheap, in part, a dirty movie, if it is a movie at all. It is a chopped up "story" of Bob Dylan's stormy visit to England. It is certainly not for moviegoers who bathe and/or shave. It is "underground" and should be buried at once. Burn a rag, as was once said of filth. Phew! *CLEVELAND PLAIN DEALER*

A relentlessly honest, brilliantly edited documentary, permeated with the troubador-poet's music....."Tell it like it is," is the battle cry of the highly probed and publicized population of sub-25 year olds, and the film does just that.

VARIETY

Bob Dylan is a 25-year old college flunk-out from Minneapolis.... The variety of audience who can best appreciate the film are likely to be bearded and small and completely in tune with Dylan's message.... The whole effect struck me as a sort of boring, off-color home movie of the neighborhoods biggest brat blowing his nose for 90 minutes.

ATLANTA (Ga.) JOURNAL

There are scenes between Dylan, Joan Baez and people in Dylan's working group, shot in the back of cars and in cluttered hotel rooms, that catch some moving essence of being young now.... Pennebaker seems to have the born filmmaker's quality of attentiveness, and the repose that allows things to occur before the camera as richly as they can in life. *THE NEW YORKER*